This book was researched and written in part by Karin Anders and edited by Susan Strawbridge, Park Services Specialist at Ellie Schiller Homosassa Springs Wildlife State Park.

Acknowledgements

The park extends its sincere gratitude to Kathy Turner Thompson, Director of Museum Services at the Citrus County Courthouse Museum; John Gannon, President of the Citrus County Historical Society; Priscilla Watkins, local historian and a member of the Homosassa Civic Club; and local resident Carlis Harman and family for their review and assistance throughout this project. We appreciate their input and suggestions. Thanks also to Gail Mitchell for reviewing the text for grammatical accuracy.

Photo Credits:

Photos have been provided through the State Library & Archives of Florida, Citrus County Historical Society, the National Gallery of Art in Washington, D.C., the Carlis Harman family and from the collection of the Ellie Schiller Homosassa Springs Wildlife State Park.

Kenneth Burchell: *Page 58, Red Wolf photo*
Jean Carter: *Page 59, Red Wolf photo*
Kelly Elliott: *page 25, photo of McRae residence*
Bill Garvin: *Page 48, hippo receiving birthday cake photo; page 53, small photo of speaker at Progress Energy event; page 62, two photos of manatees in spring; page 60, photo of Fish Bowl and manatees*
Dorothy Hahn: *Page 46, photo of hippopotamus with mouth open*
Phyllis Konitshek: *Page 58, photo of Florida panther; page 59, photo of Florida panther*
Bob Moreland: *Page 40, photo of alligator with No Swimming sign*
James Moses: *Page 50: photos of Wyland's Manatee Sanctuary mural, artist Wyland and Guy Harvey*
Susan Strawbridge: *Page 45, manatee examination; page 46, photo of J.P. Garner and Dr. Jesse White; page 49, photo of Visitor Center; page 51, photos of Wildlife Walk; page 53, photo of Wildlife Encounter pavilion and Hydrogen fuel cell installation; page 52, photo of Felburn Wildlife Care Center; page 55, photos of Ellie Schiller and park renaming event; page 63, photo of alligator; page 56, photo of flamingoes; page 60, photo of manatee program*

© 2009 Ellie Schiller Homosassa Springs Wildlife State Park
All rights reserved
No part of this publication may be reproduced in any form without permission from the publisher.

© 2009 Designed in the U.S.A. by Terrell Creative • Printed in China • 05K0091

Distributed by:
Ellie Schiller Homosassa Springs Wildlife State Park
4150 S. Suncoast Boulevard • Homosassa, Florida 34446 • (352) 628-7002

ISBN-13: 978-1-56944-392-7

In January and early February of 1904, the famous American artist Winslow Homer, attracted by its sports fishing opportunities, traveled to the Homosassa area. He stayed at the Homosassa Inn and was so enamored with the beauty of the scenery and warm climate that he was inspired to paint 11 outstanding watercolors. *The Red Shirt*, pictured here, is of a scene on the Homosassa River and is in the collection of the National Gallery of Art in Washington, D.C.

An exhibit of prints of Homer's watercolors of Homosassa and other locations in Florida and the tropics can be seen in the Visitor Center of Ellie Schiller Homosassa Springs Wildlife State Park.

Introduction
— AND —
Overview

    The Homosassa area has a long history filled with interesting characters. It has enticed people with its beauty and abundance of fish, oysters, fowl, game and plant life. This beautiful environment and spring-fed rivers were irresistible to the Timucuan and Calusa Indians. The evidence of their bounty can be seen today in the mound complex next to the Crystal River.

    Chief Tiger-Tail led the Seminoles to this area, which they named Homosassa–"place where the wild peppers grow." The Seminoles thrived in the area until the U.S. government removed them in the 1830s.

    The removal of the Native Americans opened the door for William Cooley, a resident of Florida since 1813 and a former Army surveyor with an interesting history. In 1841, Cooley acted as a leader of a colony and helped 28 settlers apply for a permit to settle Homosassa. Through the Armed Occupation Act of 1842, Cooley received 160 acres in land grants.

    He added more acreage to his holdings over several years, buying from other settlers. Cooley served as the first postmaster of Homosassa, Justice of the Peace and as County Commissioner of Fisheries in 1845. In the late 1840s, Cooley sold his lands to David Levy Yulee, paving the way for Homosassa's most prominent citizen.

The United States of America

To all to whom these Presents shall come---Greeting:

Certificate No. 28

WHEREAS, William Cooley of Hernando County Florida has deposited in the General Land Office of the United States, a Certificate of the Register of the Land Office at Newnansville whereby it appears that, full payment has been made by the said William Cooley according to the provisions of the Act of Congress of the 24th of April, 1820, entitled, "An Act making further provision for the Sale of Public Lands," and the Acts supplemental thereto, for the South west quarter of the north west quarter of section twenty seven in Township twenty South of Range seventeen east in the District of Lands subject to sale at Newnansville, Florida, containing thirty nine acres and eighty one hundredths of an Acre

according to the official Plat of the Survey of the said Lands, returned to the General Land Office by the Surveyor-General, which said tract has been purchased by the said William Cooley

NOW, KNOW YE, That the United States of America, in consideration of the premises, and in conformity with the several Acts of Congress, in such cases made and provided, have given and granted, and by these presents do give and grant unto the said William Cooley above described; To have and to hold the same, together with all the rights, privileges, immunities and appurtenances, of whatsoever nature thereunto belonging, unto the said William Cooley and to his heirs and assigns, forever.

IN TESTIMONY WHEREOF, I, James K. Polk, President of the United States of America, have caused these Letters to be made Patent, and the Seal of the General Land Office to be hereunto affixed.

Given under my hand, at the City of Washington, the first day of July in the year of our Lord one thousand eight hundred and forty-eight and of the Independence of the United States, the one hundred and seventy second.

BY THE PRESIDENT: James K. Polk
By J. K. Stephens Ass't. Secretary.

S. H. Laughlin Recorder of the General Land Office.

Recorded, Vol. _____ Page _____
Recorded this 25 day of May A.D. 1926.

Claude Connor Clerk Court.
Marguerite Bridges Deputy.

Ellie Schiller Homosassa Springs Wildlife State Park: Then and Now   5

    In 1848, U.S. Senator, entrepreneur, statesman and visionary, David Levy Yulee acquired about 5,000 acres of land including the spring and established in 1851 a sugar cane plantation, which he named Margarita. The house was located on Tiger Tail Island. A sugar boiling factory, commonly called the Sugar Mill, was built about three miles upriver and still stands today as the focal point of the Yulee Sugar Mill State Park.

    He served one term in the U.S. Senate, but when his second bid for a seat was unsuccessful, it freed him to pursue his dream of building a railroad across Florida to move products from Jacksonville-Fernandina ports to New Orleans through Pensacola, Tampa and Havana. He established the Florida Railroad Company in 1853, which began construction in 1855. The first train arrived in Cedar Key a few weeks before the start of the Civil War in 1861. According to Florida Railroad Company papers, the line was 155.5 miles long and included cars that could carry passengers, mail and freight.

Tiger Tail Island and remains of Yulee's home

It is estimated that this photo was taken between 1910 and 1920. It shows William D. and Maude Harman in the boat and their children wading in the river alongside Tiger Tail Island. In 1896, Mr. Harman had moved the family to Tiger Tail Island from Tompkinsville (now Inverness).

Ruins of David Levy Yulee's home can be seen still standing on Tiger Tail Island.

The David Yulee Sugar Mill - Built 1839 - Homosassa, Fla.

    Yulee was elected a second time to the U.S. Senate in 1855. He resigned on January 21, 1861, to join the Confederacy at the start of the American Civil War. His sugar mill supplied sugar to the Confederate Army until 1864 when Union troops blocked transport from the mill and burned the home, Margarita. Yulee was arrested in Gainesville, May 25, 1865, and imprisoned in Fort Pulaski for supporting the Confederate Army. He was pardoned by President Andrew Johnson after serving ten months.

    The Yulee Sugar Mill was deeded to the state by the Florida Federation of Women's Clubs in 1953. Open to the public, it is located on Yulee Drive in Homosassa.

    Cedar and cypress trees were in abundant supply in the forests of Homosassa from the 1840s on, providing good income as the wood was in high demand. The huge logs were rafted up the river and then loaded onto oxen carts to be delivered to cedar mills in Crystal River, Cedar Key and Homosassa.

    Cedar became a large industry and provided stable work for many. The largest mill in the area was Foster Cedar Mill.

    The cypress tree shown here is representative of the giant trees that were found throughout the area.

Built in the 1880s on the northern bank of the Homosassa River, the Rendezvous Hotel was used by wealthy men who were drawn to the area for its legendary fishing and hunting opportunities. It was built by John Stetson, famous hat maker, and Francis Bangs, law partner to Grover Cleveland. The hotel was torn down in the 1960s.

HARRY DUTTON.
TREMONT & BEACON STREETS,
BOSTON.

December 5th, 1908.

Dear Lee:-
  Enclosed please find bill of lading for mattress and dog crate. You will see by the enclosed bill that the freight is prepaid through to Homosassa, so there should be no charge whatever on this freight.
  If nothing happens to prevent, I shall leave here on Monday, December 28th, arriving at Homosassa, Wednesday night, December 30th. Please be at Homosassa with horses all ready so that I can go shooting on Thursday.
  With kind regards, I am,
    Very truly yours,
    Harry Dutton

  In 1886, three northern financiers, Joshua Chamberlain, Benjamin Dutton and John Dunn, formed the Homosassa Land Company. They bought most of the riverfront property once owned by Yulee with the intentions of building a premiere vacation spot. They were instrumental in bringing the railroad into Homosassa.
  Dutton also built the Homosassa Riverside Lodge, which was later demolished in the 1960s by the Norris Development Company.

The journey by land to reach Homosassa was difficult before 1888; famous and wealthy sportsmen would travel by train to Ocala. Then they would transfer to horse and buggy for the remaining 40 miles to Homosassa. The avid outdoorsmen were then delivered into the area by drivers. The photo shown above is of Harry Dutton's caretaker with a typical horse and buggy.

BIG BLUE SPRING, HOMOSASSA RIVER, FLA.

    A rare phenomenon occurs at the headwaters of the Homosassa River. Thousands of fresh and saltwater fish comingle in the brackish waters. Manatees are also attracted to the area and travel between the spring and the Gulf of Mexico, nine miles away.
    People have always been enticed to the clear spring waters of the Homosassa River, some even believing that they have healing powers.
    The picture on the above 1913 postcard shows local residents enjoying a day of fishing.

The old palmetto school house was an early school in the 1900s. Many of the early schools were made out of palmetto thatch in Florida as it was an abundant material. This island school was located on Gordy Island along the Homosassa River.

    The children were picked up from their homes on many of the neighboring islands by this boat piloted by two unidentified gentlemen. Teachers Katie Lashley and Rosa Campbell taught in Ozello and then later in Homosassa. The smaller photo shows Katie Lashley paddling her boat to gather students from their island homes to bring them to the Ozello School.

16 Ellie Schiller Homosassa Springs Wildlife State Park: Then and Now

Homosassa Train Depot by Joseph C. Newton, artist

Artist Joseph C. Newton completed this ink rendering of the Homosassa Train Depot from old photos taken in the 1920s.

Homosassa's Mullet Train

In 1888, the railroad extension from Ocala to Homosassa began operation. The steam locomotive, mail car, two passenger cars and a flatbed car ran daily and made the wonders of Homosassa more accessible to tourists and businessmen alike.

The train depot was built in 1893 on what is now called Yulee Drive. Engine 501 from Homosassa earned the nickname *The Mullet Train* because it transported approximately 1,200 barrels of fish each day.

Commercial fishing became profitable since the river was filled with mullet and other fish. Some fishermen who netted for mullet also acted as fishing guides to wealthy sportsmen to supplement their incomes. Homosassa's amazing sport fishing opportunities were getting noticed.

The area continued to attract many affluent sportsmen who traveled to Homosassa for the fishing and hunting and to enjoy the area's picturesque unspoiled beauty.

The popularity of the area allowed more economic and residential development. Entrepreneurs established businesses that provided stable jobs for the community, while outdoor enthusiasts continued to come to the area to fish, hunt and to enjoy its inns and lodges.

Atlanta Fishing Club, Homosassa, Fla.

The Atlantic Fishing Club appears today much as it did when it was built by a group of wealthy sportsmen from Atlanta. The group obtained a charter in 1904 with 24 founding members. It continues as a private club with a maximum of 50 members. These sports fishermen seek trophy tarpon, snook, redfish and trout.

Walk Over The Homosassa Springs

   Bruce Hoover, a Chicago businessman and developer of Homosassa Springs, known to local residents as "New Homosassa," visited the area in 1924. He fell instantly in love with the area and its beautiful natural spring. He constructed the first bridge over the spring, which was known to locals as the Fish Bowl.
   He is said to have remarked to the carpenters upon the completion of the walkway, "I hope mankind will never see fit to destroy this spring, nor enclose it behind iron gates from the eyes of the world. For only God could create such a majestic sight. For truly it is a wonder of the world and a natural bowl of fish."

The Florida West Coast Development Company built the Homosassa Hotel in the early 1920s as part of a grand vision for a "New" Homosassa. They aggressively advertised and proposed a community development plan that interested many investors and prospective property owners. However, their dream never fully materialized as economic difficulties hit Homosassa and the entire nation after the Florida land boom went bust in the late 1920s.

John Dunn, land developer, banker and phosphate pioneer, built the three-room cottage as his second private residence. After additions, it became an inn in 1890. In 1894, it was sold to Captain Alfred E. Willard and his wife, Helen. John Jacob Astor, Winslow Homer and Thomas Edison were all guests of the inn.

James and Mary MacRae purchased the Homosassa Inn in 1919 with the provision that the previous owner, Helen Richardson, be permitted to live there until her death. The MacRaes reopened the house as a lodge in 1932 and later added a second story after World War II. It reverted back to their residence in 1994.

This circa 1945 photo shows the owner of Nature's Giant Fish Bowl, David Newell, welcoming Sally Kennedy of the Florida Outdoor Writers Association. Mr. Newell, the author of four books on Central Florida and host of the radio program *The Hunting and Fishing Club of the Air*, was also the editor of *Field & Stream* magazine. He promoted this new attraction to outdoor enthusiasts throughout the world.

David Newell of Leesburg, Florida, acquired the property in the 1940s and developed an attraction around the main spring, which he called Nature's Giant Fish Bowl. The attraction was opened to the public in 1945. To compete successfully with other river attractions and their glass bottom boats, Newell added a three-story wooden observatory over the spring with an underwater walkway for better views of the natural phenomenon of fresh and saltwater fish in the headwaters. In 1945, Newell formed the Homosassa River Corporation as the owner of the property.

Local resident Elmo Reed purchased the attraction from Newell in 1950 and operated it until 1962, when it was sold to millionaire Chicago businessman Bruce Norris of Norris Development. He renamed it Homosassa Springs, Nature's Own Attraction.

Dazzy Vance, "The Old Dazzler," and Citrus County's favorite big leaguer, loved to fish, and that is why he came to Citrus County in the first place. Here he is in 1931 with a fine mess of fish.

He purchased the Homosassa Hotel in the fall of 1930 and spent his winters here and his summers playing baseball with the Brooklyn Dodgers. He was elected to the Baseball Hall of Fame in 1955 and died at his home in Homosassa on February 16, 1961. He is buried in Stage Stand Cemetery, alongside U.S. 19, just south of town. The hotel was torn down in the 1960s to build a shopping center.

In 1951, *Crosswinds*, an adventure movie starring John Payne, Rhonda Fleming and Forrest Tucker, began filming in Homosassa. The area served as an important backdrop for the film, as treasure hunters searched for sunken government gold.

The photo at right shows Rhonda Fleming and John Payne standing and an unidentified actor sitting. Since then, many other films and television documentaries have been filmed in Homosassa Springs.

Postal service was first established in Homosassa in 1845, but was discontinued several times. In 1886, the post office was re-established and was located in homes or businesses for many years. The building pictured here served as the post office from 1947 to 1968 and was located where Gulf Coast Marine is now across from the school. Constructed out of Sabal palm logs, it was built by Willie Adkins, father of Russell Adkins, Postmaster from 1947 to 1967.

The alligators at Homosassa's Gator Lagoon have been popular since the 1940s. In the early days of the attraction, visitors watched the large reptiles jump for fish and chicken offered by animal handlers.

Now, as a Florida State Park, the emphasis is on environmental education, focusing on native Florida's wildlife. Alligators are no longer fed during programs to avoid giving the wrong message to visitors.

A new fish bowl underwater observatory was installed in late 1963 and opened in early 1964. General Manager G.A. Furgason came up with the idea of a newer and larger underwater observatory. Construction was done north of Ocala and then transported to Homosassa for assembly.

This photo shows the Fish Bowl as it appeared then with its colorful canopy. The Fish Bowl Observatory floats within the spring and provides a view of the marine life from an underwater room with wraparound windows.

POPULAR MECHANICS

JAN. 1965
35 CENTS

Bananas Launch Fish Observatory

FACED WITH THE TASK of launching a 157-ton underwater observatory into a natural aquarium, the managers of Homosassa Springs, an aquatic showcase on Florida's gulf coast, covered the ways with a lubricant that was both slippery enough and harmless to fish—ripe bananas.

Like the underside of an iceberg, the windowed observatory hangs beneath a roomy sundeck. Twelve thousand dollars worth of two-inch glass gives observers a panoramic view of the 55-foot deep natural spring, which is noted for its teeming population of various fresh and salt water fish. The observatory was custom designed for the Norris Development Co., owners of Homosassa Springs, to highlight this unique mixture of fish species.

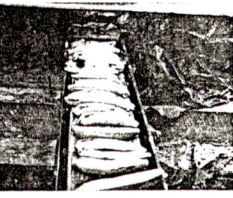

GREASING THE WAYS for the launching of the underwater observatory called for lubricant harmless to the wide variety of tropical fish. It was edible, too

TAKING A TIP from old Max Sennett film comedies, owners of Homosassa observatory covered launching skids with a safe and slippery lubricant—bananas

BALANCED BY A CRANE, the observatory slides down the banana-greased ways and into the water. The slanted windows give the best possible viewing angle

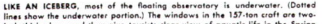
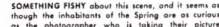

LIKE AN ICEBERG, most of the floating observatory is underwater. (Dotted lines show the underwater portion.) The windows in the 157-ton craft are two-inch-thick glass, and they give tourists clear view of aquatic life in the Spring

SOMETHING FISHY about this scene, and it seems as though the inhabitants of the Spring are as curious as the photographer who is taking their picture

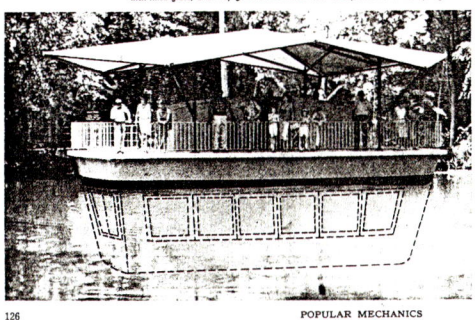
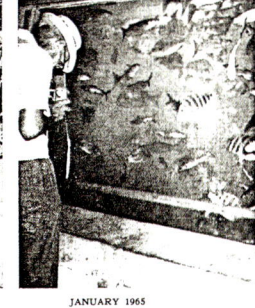

126   POPULAR MECHANICS   JANUARY 1965

Banana peels were used to grease the rails during the launch of the 168-ton structure so as not to disturb the ecology of the spring. A Max Sennett movie was credited with the innovative idea. *Popular Mechanics* featured a full-page article on the Fish Bowl's launching.

Harry Wainwright (right) shows off a nice catch from a day out on the river. Fish nets are shown above drying out on the Homosassa River.

34 Ellie Schiller Homosassa Springs Wildlife State Park: Then and Now

The Homosassa area was truly a sportsman's paradise. Pictured here are (left to right) – Harry Wainwright, Newton Henley, T.L. Rodgers, James A. MacRae and Scott Finley.

Dick Wainwright is shown aboard the *Shirley Ann* getting ready to head out on the Homosassa River for a day of fishing.

Tiny, the chimpanzee, and Clarence, the cross-eyed lion, are pictured here posing for a publicity photo for the Homosassa Springs Attraction.

Homosassa Springs Attraction housed Ivan Tours Animal Actors between movie and television appearances. Buck, the bear, who played Gentle Ben; Clarence, the cross-eyed lion from *Daktari*; Tiny and Freckles, the chimpanzees; Flipper, the dolphin, and the Exxon tiger were some of the famous animals who stayed at the park. Lu, the hippopotamus, also came to Homosassa Springs Attraction as part of Ivan Tours Animal Actors.

Scrapbook of The Early Days of Homosassa Springs Attraction

38 Ellie Schiller Homosassa Springs Wildlife State Park: Then and Now

Ellie Schiller Homosassa Springs Wildlife State Park: Then and Now

40 Ellie Schiller Homosassa Springs Wildlife State Park: Then and Now

Homosassa Springs continued to operate as an exotic wildlife attraction through the 1970s and 1980s. Pictured at left is one of the attraction's brochures and above, the famous "Don't Miss Homosassa Springs" billboard with one of the Indian maidens.

This color map of the attraction adorned the back of the snack bar menu, while the fish identification booklets were a popular item in the gift shops.

42 Ellie Schiller Homosassa Springs Wildlife State Park: Then and Now

After purchasing Homosassa Springs in 1963, Bruce Norris dredged Pepper Creek and added pontoon boats to transport visitors on a jungle cruise from the main entrance on U.S. 19 to the entrance on Fish Bowl Drive.

44 Ellie Schiller Homosassa Springs Wildlife State Park: Then and Now

The attraction went through several changes in ownership during the late 1970s and 1980s. When Taylor Simpson purchased the attraction on December 1, 1984, he renamed it Homosassa Springs Nature World and made J.P. Garner the Attraction Manager.

In the photo above, veterinarians and wildlife care staff from Homosassa Springs Nature World and Sea World examine a manatee before it is moved into the spring. J.P. Garner is in the front wearing the blue, grey and black wetsuit. Betsy Dearth is standing on the far right.

Ellie Schiller Homosassa Springs Wildlife State Park: Then and Now

J.P. Garner, Manager Nature World Attraction

Dr. Jesse White with Ranger, a newborn manatee calf

    During this period of time, veterinarian Dr. Jesse White from Miami Seaquarium visited the attraction and discussed with Taylor Simpson and J.P. Garner the possibility of Homosassa Springs Nature World becoming a halfway house for orphaned manatees and those recovering from injuries before they would be released into the wild. They agreed that the headwaters and spring run would make the ideal environment for recovering manatees since it offered a natural habitat for this transition period.

46   Ellie Schiller Homosassa Springs Wildlife State Park: Then and Now

Becoming a Florida State Park

SAVING THE SPRINGS

In early 1984, Simpson came to a decision to sell Homosassa Springs Nature World. He soon received offers from parties interested in purchasing the property for development as an R.V. park or for condominiums. Local residents who didn't want to lose this natural treasure formed the grass roots group, Citizens to Save Our Springs, and circulated and collected petitions to encourage the County to purchase the land until the State of Florida would be able to purchase it and preserve it as a Florida state park. These petitions were presented to the Board of County Commissioners, who decided to put it on a special referendum to Citrus County voters to decide the attraction's fate.

The referendum for the county to purchase the property passed by less than 200 votes on September 4, 1984. Citrus County took over the temporary ownership and operation of the attraction for three years until December 31, 1988. In April 1985, the attraction property was accepted by the site selection committee for the Conservation and Recreational Lands (CARL) program. The attraction officially became a Florida state park on January 1, 1989, with its new name becoming Homosassa Springs Wildlife State Park. The state began widespread improvements throughout the property. The emphasis changed from entertainment to education with the focus from exotic animals to native Florida wildlife.

On January 1, 1989, the state of Florida took over operation of the former attraction as a Florida state park. Homosassa Springs Wildlife State Park would now showcase Florida's native wildlife. As the park sought to find new homes for the exotic animals in the collection, local citizens sent letters to the local newspaper requesting that the popular hippopotamus, Lu, be allowed to stay on at the park. Thousands of letters were sent to Governor Lawton Chiles, who decided to make Lu an honorary citizen of the State of Florida and allow him to live out his life at Homosassa Springs. Every January the wildlife park celebrates Lu's birthday with a birthday cake and invites area school children to a party. Park Manager Art Yerian is shown giving Lu his cake.

In 1993, the state of Florida purchased the property on U.S. 19 including the Visitor Center and boat docks. Pontoon boats transported park visitors down Pepper Creek to the wildlife park and the west entrance where they explored the wildlife park.

Ellie Schiller Homosassa Springs Wildlife State Park: Then and Now   49

Wyland, along with artist Guy Harvey, painted a 55-foot-long mural along the south wall of the Homosassa Springs Wildlife State Park's Visitor Center. This is the 86th Whaling Wall painted by the environmental artist. The life-size mural features the endangered West Indian manatees and depicts some of the fish found in the spring. The mural, entitled *Manatee Sanctuary*, was dedicated on October 23, 2000, and has been enjoyed by all who visit the park.

Artists Wyland and Guy Harvey posed for a photo while painting the mural above.

The Wildlife Walk represented one of the most significant improvements made to the park since it became a state park. This project provided our resident wildlife with large open exhibits and our visitors with an elevated boardwalk for improved access and viewing opportunities. It was completed in two phases with a grand opening on March 27, 2004.

Ellie Schiller Homosassa Springs Wildlife State Park: Then and Now   51

In 2005, construction began on the park's new 8,000-square-foot Felburn Wildlife Care Center funded by a grant from the Felburn Foundation, which was then matched by the state of Florida as a Partnership in Parks project.

The center encompasses a commissary for preparation of animal diets, a veterinary clinic, offices, intern/biologist/researcher housing for up to four persons and a wildlife quarantine section. The new facility was completed with a grand opening on September 24, 2008. It provides state-of-the-art technology to help care for and aid in the recovery of endangered wildlife including West Indian manatees, black bears, cougars and whooping cranes.

An innovative hydrogen fuel cell was installed by Progress Energy at the Wildlife Encounter Pavilion in 2005. This educational exhibit also helps to provide energy to the Pavilion. Additional solar panels at the Visitor Center help provide some power needs on the boat docks.

Ellie Schiller Homosassa Springs Wildlife State Park: Then and Now   53

MANATEE CARE CENTER
for Treatment and Research

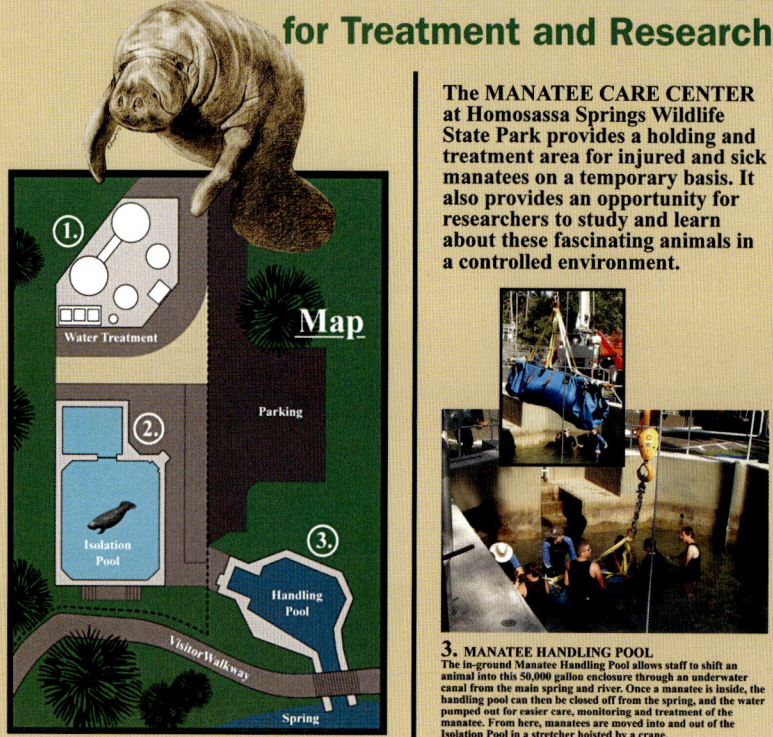

The **MANATEE CARE CENTER** at Homosassa Springs Wildlife State Park provides a holding and treatment area for injured and sick manatees on a temporary basis. It also provides an opportunity for researchers to study and learn about these fascinating animals in a controlled environment.

1. WATER TREATMENT SYSTEM
Here is contained the system of pumps and filters for operating the 65,000 gallon Manatee Isolation Pool. Water is heated for the animals' comfort during the winter season.

2. MANATEE ISOLATION POOL
The Manatee Isolation Pool is an above ground facility divided into two areas, one of which has a moveable floor. Staff members can raise the floor, effectively raising the manatee out of the water, so they can provide medical and routine husbandry care on a dry surface. Up to five manatees at a time can be placed within the isolation pool area.

3. MANATEE HANDLING POOL
The in-ground Manatee Handling Pool allows staff to shift an animal into this 50,000 gallon enclosure through an underwater canal from the main spring and river. Once a manatee is inside, the handling pool can then be closed off from the spring, and the water pumped out for easier care, monitoring and treatment of the manatee. From here, manatees are moved into and out of the Isolation Pool in a stretcher hoisted by a crane.

Homosassa Springs Wildlife State Park is one of the only three designated manatee secondary recovery facilities in the world. It is famous as a rehabilitation center and refuge for injured and orphaned manatees.

July 15, 2009, the park was officially renamed in honor of Ellie Schiller. A special event was held in the Garden of the Springs during which a replica of the park's new sign was unveiled.

Ellie Schiller was a generous and faithful supporter of Homosassa Springs Wildlife State Park. As Director of the Felburn Foundation, she enthusiastically contributed to many major projects at the wildlife park including the new black bear exhibit, both phases of the wildlife walk, a new roseate spoonbill aviary, new red wolves habitat and housing and improvements to the wildlife habitats for the Florida panther, birds of prey, foxes and otters. Most recently through the Felburn Foundation, her generous donation to the Friends of Homosassa Springs Wildlife Park, Inc., raised the funds necessary to apply for matching state funds as a Partnership in Parks project.

Ms. Schiller loved wildlife and nature, and she loved this park. Her support helped to make this park a showcase for native Florida's wildlife. Park Manager Art Yerian notes, "With Ellie Schiller's support we've been able to accomplish projects that are a natural extension of our mission to help preserve and protect wildlife at Homosassa Springs Wildlife State Park."

Scrapbook of Ellie Schiller Homosassa Springs Wildlife State Park Today

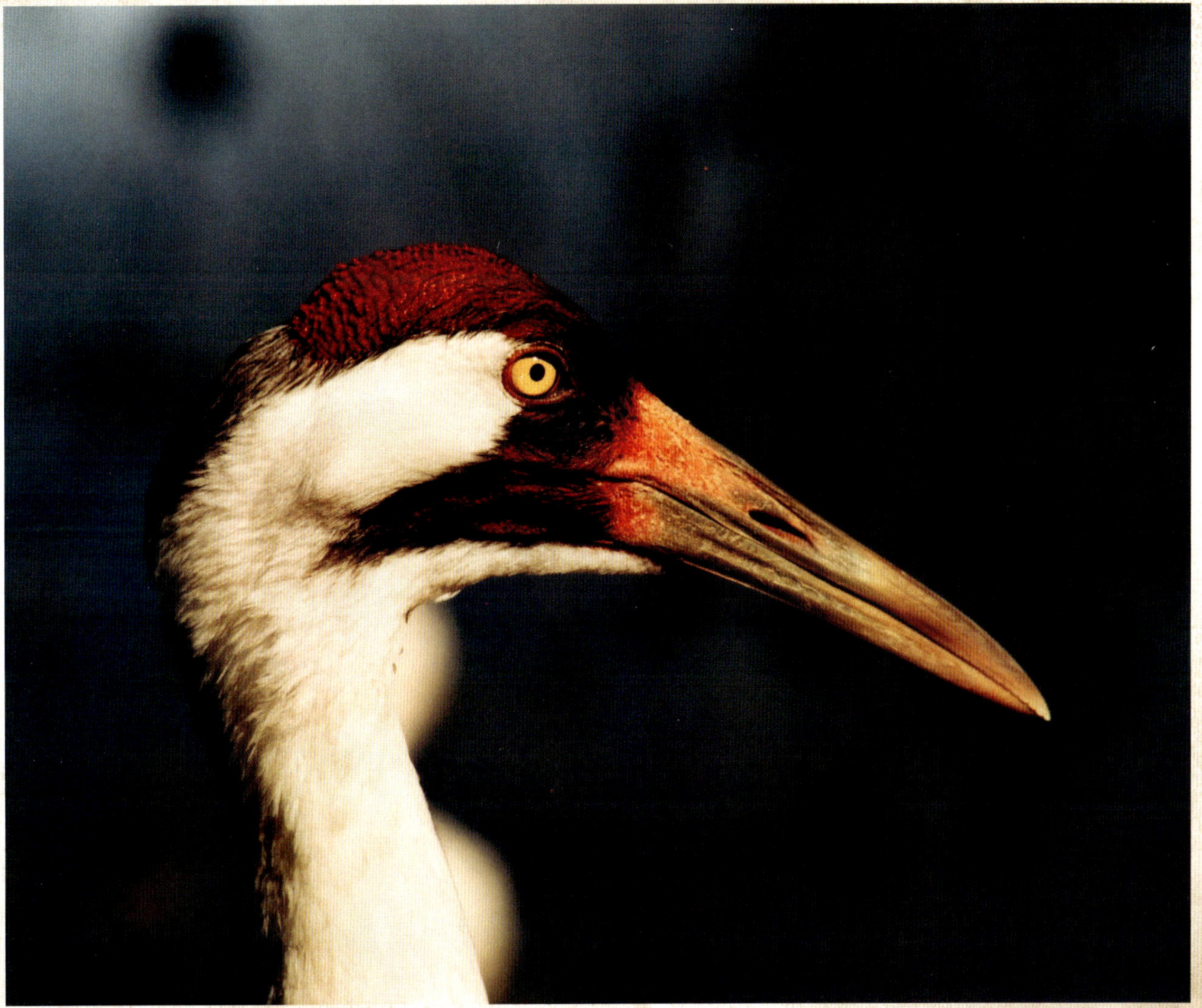

The Wildlife Park is now home to several endangered species through partnerships with agencies including the U.S. Fish and Wildlife Service and Florida Fish and Wildlife Conservation Commission. Whooping cranes, red wolves and a Florida panther are among the species represented.

Ellie Schiller Homosassa Springs Wildlife State Park: Then and Now   59

60   Ellie Schiller Homosassa Springs Wildlife State Park: Then and Now

Ellie Schiller Homosassa Springs Wildlife State Park: Then and Now

Educational programs on the West Indian manatees are offered three times daily at the park. In addition to the resident manatees at Ellie Schiller Homosassa Springs Wildlife State Park, wild manatees are attracted to the area and are seen often, especially during the winter months. These gentle mammals can grow to be 13 feet in length and weigh more than 3,000 pounds.

Ellie Schiller Homosassa Springs Wildlife State Park: Then and Now

Bibliography

Carter, W. Horace, *Nature's Masterpiece of Homosassa: Where the Saltgrass Joins the Sawgrass.* Atlantic Publishing Company, Tabor City, NC 1981.

Dunn, Hampton, *Back Home: A History of Citrus County, Florida:* Citrus County Bicentennial Steering Committee, Inverness, FL 1976.

Foulk, K. M., "History of the Homosassa Inn."

Hollis, Tim, *Glass Bottom Boats and Mermaid Tails.* Stackpole Books, Mechanicsburg, PA 2006.

Homan, Lynn M. and Thomas Riley, *Images of America: Citrus County.* Arcadia Publishing, Charleston, SC 2001.

Knetsch, Joseph, "William Cooley and the Beginnings of the Homosassa Settlement." *At Home* newsletter of the Citrus County Historical Society, March/April 1999.

State Library & Archives of Florida's *Florida Memory* electronic library on the web

www.citrus.fl.org/derservice/commdev. Appendix H retrieved 2003.

www.member.cox.net/gvick/history.html. Retrieved 2008.

www.tfn.net/springs/Homosassa.html.

A Message from the Park Manager

We hope you enjoy this pictorial history of our community and our park from its early days as an attraction to its current role as a Florida State Park showcasing Florida's wildlife. We invite you to visit Ellie Schiller Homosassa Springs Wildlife State Park and enjoy what our park has to offer.
Art Yerian, Park Manager